FROM PAYCHECK TO PROSPERITY

From Paycheck to Prosperity

Eksha Agrawal

Copyright © 2024 by Eksha Agrawal

All rights reserved. No part of this book may be reproduced in any manner whatsoever without written permission except in the case of brief quotations embodied in critical articles and reviews.

First Printing, 2024

Contents

Dedication vii
Acknowledgment ix
Foreword xi

SECTION 1: ELEMENTS OF PERSONAL FINANCE MANAGEMENT 1
  1 Importance of Personal Finance Management 3
  2 Tools to Manage Personal Finances 7
  3 Achieving Goals with Personal Finance Management 9
  4 How to Become Debt-Free 15
  5 How to Become Financially Free 21

SECTION 2: INVESTING IN PAPER ASSETS 27
  6 Investing in Stocks/Shares 29
  7 Investing in Mutual Funds 33
  8 How to Perform Technical and Financial Analysis 39
  9 How to Manage Your Personal Finances 47

Dedication

To my parents, *Khushbu & Ajay Agrawal*, thank you for raising me to be an independent and well-educated woman. Your love, sacrifices, and values have been the foundation of everything I've achieved. I owe it all to you.

To my teachers, for sparking curiosity and inspiring me to dream big. You didn't just teach me lessons; you shaped the way I see the world.

To my friends and peers, who've been there through thick and thin, helping me learn, laugh, and look at life with fresh perspectives. You've been my sounding boards, cheerleaders, and occasional therapists.

To my past employers, thank you for trusting me with opportunities that pushed me to grow. The lessons I've learned from you—both professionally and personally—have been invaluable.

To *Lord Brihaspati*, whose blessings have been my guiding light. I'm forever grateful for the wisdom and inspiration to share what I know with the world.

Acknowledgment

A big thank you to *Hemsingh Patle* for nudging me (well, maybe pushing me a little!) to relaunch this book. Your belief in me and this project means the world.

To *Manoj Sonawane*, who worked behind the scenes to shape this book into something I'm truly proud of. Thank you for your editing magic, patience, and for helping it reach readers far and wide.

And to everyone who has been a part of my journey—whether you've offered advice, feedback, or just a word of encouragement—this book wouldn't exist without you. Your support has been everything.

Thanks,
Eksha

Foreword

Money and wealth are two different things. One can be rich in terms of money but not wealthy. It's also true that money holds the key to your wealth because once you gain control of your money, you'll experience real wealth in terms of both 1) time, and 2) life experiences and wealthy people always find ways to be in these two distinct domains of life. They save time by using money and are open to new life experiences and that helps them to grow. But how do you gain control of your money? Let's find the answer to this question by understanding the four-step key process below.

Effective money management involves four key steps:

1. Expenditure allocation
2. Develop the habit of saving money regularly.
3. Research and choose the investment option that best suits your needs, then start investing in it.
4. Then slowly move to more other investment avenues and grow your money.

Eksha has accomplished a remarkable feat by crafting this book in a manner that is easy to comprehend and that decodes the answers to the above four-step key process. Whether you're just starting to build your financial future or looking to optimize your existing strategy, this book provides a roadmap that can be tailored to your unique needs and goals.

Inside, you'll find practical advice and actionable steps to help you take control of your finances, save more, and invest wisely. By following this structured approach, you can unlock the potential to achieve your financial goals and secure your long-term financial well-being. This is a book that I wish I had read ten years ago.

Happy Reading
Manoj Sonawane

SECTION 1: ELEMENTS OF PERSONAL FINANCE MANAGEMENT

"Being rich is having money, being wealthy is having time".
-Margaret Bonanno

1

Importance of Personal Finance Management

"You must gain control over your money or the lack of it will forever control you."

-Dave Ramsey

The onset of the coronavirus pandemic in 2020 had spiked the stress levels around the world. Stress level because of fear of disease? More than the fear of disease, people today are scared for their financial future and how they would be able to sustain the lifestyle which they have built on poor financial management.

The stress is due to the fear that the house of lifestyle which has been built on cards of multiple debts can come crashing anytime.

Many people invested in so-called "Equity linked saving schemes" and watched their hard earned invested money crash down, and were also hoping that market correction will improve their investment in future.

Is there any dearth of money in their lives?

No, I am talking about people who are earning well, who are nowhere near the poverty line and still they are so stressed about their financial future. Why?

Because we have never been taught to manage our finances.

Figure 1: We are not born just to pay our bills

College graduation, job and voila! No need to ask for pocket money from parents. Now, we earn our own bread, or should I say, pizza, beer and what not. We are never taught what to do with that sudden surge of money and we end up trapping ourselves in a vicious cycle. All because we don't know how to manage our finances. Personal financial management is the need of the hour.

Today, we need to learn it more than in any other time or generation. If we manage our finances well, we can face any difficulty or challenge with less stress and make rational decisions.

Let's find out how this vicious circle works in most of the cases. 8 out of 10 people would fall in one or more than one trap.

College (Student loan) -> Job (Credit Card) -> Car (Car loan) -> Marriage (Personal loan) -> House (Home loan) -> Kids (kids expenses) -> Retirement.

All the stages mentioned above are important stages of life, one needs to get married, have kids in order to live a happy life (at least this is what many of us want to believe), however, if we do not have our employment tomorrow, then all these plans send shivers down our spine.

So, the best way out is to learn and manage our finances.

Let's start with the chapter that covers tools to manage your personal finances.

2

Tools to Manage Personal Finances

"It's not how much money you make, but how much money you keep, how hard it works for you, and how many generations you keep it for."

-Robert Kiyosaki

Honestly, there is no rocket science behind personal finance management. It can be done on a piece of paper, or by maintaining it in a diary or any software. But, in this book, we will learn the method of maintaining expenses on a tool which I have personally found most effective, that is Microsoft Excel. Simply because, even if you bought a product 10 years ago, you can find out how much you spent on it by using this software. This utility is quite unlikely to find, if we maintain our finances in a diary.

A more advanced and readily available tool is an excel sheet available via Google drive or One drive. The ease of access is unparalleled.

I uses two google sheets to manage all my finances which I had names as:

1) Budget planning
2) Expense Sheet

We will learn more about it in subsequent chapters with examples. Some other useful tools are:

-Any EMI calculator available on the internet before taking any loan.

-The most important of all, YOUR BRAIN, use it well! Yes, that is sharper than any other tools of the world. It calculates expenses faster than any software.

In the next chapter, we will learn about how to achieve your goals with personal finance management.

3

Achieving Goals with Personal Finance Management

"*Beware of little expenses. A small leak will sink a great ship.*"

-Benjamin Franklin

In this chapter, we'll explore how to manage your finances in a way that helps you achieve personal goals, such as going on exotic vacations, purchasing a car, or planning your wedding. While these goals are often attainable through loans, there's something much more rewarding about achieving them without the burden of hefty monthly installments. Even better is when your monthly payments account for only a small portion of your income.

Achieving Your Vacation Goal

Start by creating an annual travel plan. While spontaneous trips can be fun, they often end up costing more than expected. Planning ahead not only saves you money but also offers the chance to secure cheaper flight tickets, gives you time to craft your itinerary, and lets you experience the excitement of anticipation.

To get started, decide how often you'd like to travel based on your income and interests. For example, I personally aim to travel every two months.

Here's a sample of how you can structure your travel tracker:

Month	Target City	Actual City	Budget	Actual Expenses	Remarks
Jan	City X	City X	25k	23k	Enjoyed boat ride
March	City Y	City Y	15k	20k	Hostel was worth the money
May	City Z	City A	38k	39k	Beautiful rivers
July	City A	-	20k	-	Couldn't go due to cousin's marriage
Sept	City B	-	12k	-	-
Nov	City C	-	45k	-	-

Table 1: Travel tracker

At the start of the year, outline your travel goals by selecting the cities you'd like to visit and allocate a budget for each trip. Each month, update the tracker with the actual city visited and expenses incurred. Add remarks on what went well or what could have been improved.

By keeping this tracker up-to-date, you'll have a clear view of how well you're sticking to your travel plan and what might be preventing you from reaching your goals. This also adds a fun, motivational element to your planning.

Once you have your annual plan in place, calculating the amount you need to save becomes simple: just divide your total budget by 12. For example, if your annual budget is USD 15,500 you need to save USD 1,300 every month.

This method ensures that your travel goals won't disrupt your finances, and you'll have the flexibility to adjust your plans as needed. Ideally, allocate no more than 15% of your monthly income toward travel goals.

Achieving Your Goal of Owning a Car

Owning a car is a common goal for many. It offers mobility, comfort, and a sense of status. However, sometimes our income may not be sufficient to pay for a car in full upfront. In such cases, consider saving for a down payment over six months and financing the remaining balance with EMIs for up to three years.

Ensure that your car EMIs don't exceed 15-20% of your monthly income, as car payments are a pure expense without any tax benefits.

For example, if you're looking to buy a car worth USD 70000, save USD 15000 for the down payment and finance the remaining amount via EMIs over three years. If the EMI amount exceeds 20% of your salary, it's time to reconsider or adjust the car's features. The goal is to enjoy the luxuries of life without putting yourself under financial strain.

Achieving Your Marriage Goals

Ah, marriage — a significant milestone and often seen as the "best day of your life." However, it's essential to be financially prepared, as this is a major expense without any financial returns. I recommend starting to save for your wedding at least three years in advance.

To manage your wedding budget effectively, break it down into categories. Here's a list of expenses to consider:

1. Number of guests
2. Venue
3. Catering
4. Decoration
5. Shopping and gifts
6. Photography
7. Miscellaneous expenses

Let's say your total wedding budget is USD 1,00,000. This means you'll need to save USD 2,800 per month for the next three years to meet your goal. After three years, adjustments may be necessary, but you'll be well-prepared to cover them.

Here's an example of how you can structure your savings tracker:

Month	Target Saving	Actual Saving	Remarks
January	28,00		
February	28,00		
March	28,00		
April	28,00		
May	28,00		
June	28,00		
July	28,00		
August	28,00		

September	28,00
October	28,00
November	28,00
December	28,00
Total	**336,00**

Table 2: Saving tracker

This annual tracker will help you stay on track for the next three years. It's also useful to keep another tracker for your wedding bookings and expenses, like so:

Category	**Target Budget**	**Actual Expense**	**Remarks**
Venue			
Catering			
Decoration			
Photography			
Wedding Dress			
Gifts			
Contingency			
Total			

Table 3: Wedding Expenses Tracker

These trackers act as anchors, helping you stay disciplined and focused on achieving your goals. Consistency is key — update them regularly and stay committed to your savings plan.

In the next chapter, we'll dive deeper into the importance of being debt-free — one of the most critical aspects of financial health.

4

How to Become Debt-Free

"*Wealth is the ability to fully experience life.*"

-Henry David Thoreau

Repaying Student Debt

This chapter is especially close to my heart, as I have personally navigated the challenges of student debt and emerged victorious. When I was pursuing my engineering course, I had big dreams for myself. However, my father, with limited financial resources, couldn't support my expensive education. I thought taking out a loan would solve everything, as loans were easy to obtain. What I didn't know, however, was how student loans work—the interest rates, the long-term consequences, and the financial pitfalls that come with them. At the time, my financial understanding was, frankly, non-existent.

I didn't question the loan terms or consider the long-term impact of the debt. No one guided me on how to manage repayments effectively, and I only realized the significance of early payments after the interest had already compounded significantly.

Here are some essential points to consider if you're taking a student loan:

1. **Negotiate the Interest Rate** – If possible, negotiate with the bank to freeze the interest rate in writing. I started my loan at a 9.5% rate (with a 0.25% discount for females) but ended up paying 11.75% interest due to rate fluctuations. Always understand how your interest rate can change.
2. **Start Repaying Early** – Even a small monthly repayment (e.g., USD 50 or 100) will help keep the interest in check. The earlier you start, the less interest you will pay over time.
3. **Discipline in Repayment** – Consistency is key. I had to adjust my lifestyle, cutting down expenses significantly to allocate up to 60% of my salary and yearly bonus towards loan repayment. Although it was tough, I made sure to indulge occasionally. The aim is to pay off your student debt as quickly as possible, since there are limited tax benefits associated with it, but you can claim a tax rebate on the interest.

Here's a tracker to keep tabs on your student debt repayment:

Month	Income	EMI Amount	Saving	Investing	Expenses
Jan	X	25%X	25%X	25%X	25%X
Feb	X	25%X	25%X	25%X	25%X
To	...	...	...	...	...
Dec	Y	25%Y	25%Y	25%Y	25%Y

Table 4: Target tracker

Month	Income	EMI Amount	Saving	Investing	Expenses
Jan	X	25%X	25%X	15%X	35%X
Feb	X	25%X	25%X	25%X	25%X
To	...	...	...	...	...
Dec	Y	25%Y	25%Y	25%Y	25%Y

Table 5: Actual target tracker

Maintain this tracker on an annual basis, and if you receive bonuses or other extra income, allocate them proportionally to the categories listed. The goal is to balance saving, investing, and debt repayment.

Repaying Car Loan

Car loans are a form of debt with no tax benefits, unless the vehicle is used for business purposes. These loans should be repaid as soon as possible. When considering a car purchase, ensure that the total cost doesn't exceed 60% of your annual salary, with a 40% down payment. This ensures that your car purchase doesn't negatively impact other financial goals. Don't forget to factor in insurance, warranties, and loan interest when calculating the total cost.

Use a budget tracker to keep a clear picture of how much you need to pay:

Annual Budget Tracker:

Total Car Price	X	Down Payment	Y	Loan Amount	Z

Month	Target EMI	Actual EMI
Jan	...	...
To	...	...
Dec	...	...

Table 6: Annual budget tracker

Repaying Credit Card Bill

A credit card is a powerful tool when used responsibly, but it can quickly lead to financial chaos if not managed carefully. While it offers flexibility, rewards, and the ability to improve your credit score, it can also encourage impulsive spending. Set a clear budget for credit card purchases and pay off the outstanding balance on time to maintain a healthy credit score and avoid paying high-interest charges.

Here's a monthly tracker to help you manage your credit card spending:

Budget: USD 1,000

Item	Amount
Shoes	300
Flight Tickets	500

Cosmetics	50
Gift for Mom	100
Stationary	50

Table 7: Monthly Tracker for managing your credit card spending

Due Date: DD-MM-YYYY
Total Payment: USD 1000

Update this tracker at the beginning of each month, and make sure to pay your balance by the due date. Be mindful of online frauds by keeping passwords secure and reading up on ways to prevent fraud.

Repaying Home Loan

A home loan is the most beneficial form of debt due to the income tax exemption on both the principal and interest payments. Moreover, as your income rises and the value of the property appreciates over time, the fixed rate of the loan helps offset inflation. However, avoid getting into long-term debt with no clear exit plan, as it can lead to unnecessary financial stress.

Before taking a home loan, consider the following:

1. **Income Tax Benefits** – Understand the tax savings you'll gain over the loan's tenure.
2. **EMI as a Percentage of Income** – Ensure that the EMI remains manageable relative to your income, even with potential increases.
3. **Mitigation Plan** – Have a plan in place in case your primary income stream stops.

If your salary increases regularly, repaying your home loan can be a great way to build assets while benefiting from tax savings.

Repaying Personal Loan

Personal loans, often used for weddings, medical emergencies, or other urgent needs, typically carry high interest rates (12-20%) with no tax benefits. These should be repaid as quickly as possible. Allocate at least 20% of your income towards repayment and track it using a simple monthly EMI tracker, similar to the ones discussed earlier.

Once you become debt-free, your next step is achieving **financial freedom**—creating passive income streams that cover your expenses without the need to work actively. Let's dive into that in the next chapter.

5

How to Become Financially Free

"There is only one success—to be able to spend your life in your own way."

- Christopher Morley

Achieving financial freedom and becoming debt-free are two distinct goals. Financial freedom occurs when you no longer need to work for money because your passive income exceeds your expenses. On the other hand, debt freedom focuses on eliminating liabilities. Similarly, saving for early retirement and saving to invest are different pursuits, and each serves a unique purpose depending on your life goals. While one is about embracing a minimalist lifestyle, the other is about maximizing your wealth. Let's explore these two approaches in detail.

SAVE FOR EARLY RETIREMENT

Early retirement has become a popular goal for many, with individuals retiring in their 40s or 50s. However, achieving early retirement requires careful planning. The concept behind early retirement is simple: save enough money from your job or business so that your expenses are covered without needing to work anymore.

Here's the key: you need to determine your baseline living expenses and calculate how much money is required to maintain your lifestyle without working. For example, if your current monthly expenses are INR 30,000 (USD 353) and you assume a 7% annual inflation rate, retiring at 40 and living until 70 would require a corpus of INR 3.5 crore (USD 4,11,994). As you can see, the amount needed for retirement is directly linked to your monthly expenses and your desired retirement age.

Don't be daunted by the large sum. With disciplined saving and planning, this goal is achievable. However, this path aligns with a minimalist approach—if you're someone who enjoys luxury cars, gadgets, and other material possessions, early retirement may not be the right goal for you. The primary motivation behind early retirement is the freedom it provides—the freedom to spend your time however you wish.

Let's say you start working at 22 and aim to retire by 40 (18 years later). You would need to save INR 50,000 (USD 588) per month, assuming a 12% annual return on investment, to reach INR 3.5 crore (USD 4,11,994) in 18 years. Keep in mind that your income is likely to increase over time, so you can start with a smaller monthly investment and increase it as your income grows. The key is to consistently save 60-70% of your income toward this goal.

Maintain the following annual savings tracker to keep yourself on track:

Month	Target Saving Amount	Actual Saving Amount
January		
February		

March		
To	...	...
December		
Total		

Table 8: Annual saving tracker

Value at the end of Year 1:
By following this annual tracker for the next 18 years, you'll be well on your way to meeting your goal. In fact, you may reach it even sooner! While minor setbacks are inevitable, stay focused and continue tracking your progress. Who knows—the next early retirement success story could be yours.

SAVE TO INVEST

This is my personal favorite approach—earning from any source of income and investing a portion of it in assets that will generate future income. The key is to invest regularly in the right channels. Let's take a closer look at the various investment opportunities available:

1. **Investing in Real Estate:**

Real estate remains one of the most popular investment options globally. For instance, I had a small unused space at home that my father decided to turn into a room. Initially, there were no takers. After investing in furnishings and listing the property online, we found a tenant within a month. Now, we have a steady stream of income and expect to break even in five years, after which all income will be profit.

This illustrates the power of investing with a strategy. It can also improve your problem-solving skills as you figure out ways to maximize your return on investment (ROI). You can invest in real estate either for rental income or capital appreciation. Real estate investment bonds, which combine elements of paper money investment, are also gaining popularity.

The key is to make investing a habit. Start with small, consistent investments and gradually increase your commitment. Over time, you'll find that your investments provide an additional income source, an asset to fall back on in tough times.

1. **Investing in Paper Money (Stocks, Bonds, Mutual Funds):**

Investing in paper money offers flexibility, as you can start with a small amount. Instruments like mutual funds, stocks, bonds, REITs (Real Estate Investment Trusts), and even bitcoin provide opportunities to grow your wealth. Start by investing in companies you believe in or use frequently. For example, I've adopted the rule that whenever I shop for a product from a particular company, I'll buy an equivalent amount of its stock. This helps you track performance and potentially earn profits over time.

If you're new to investing, there are plenty of courses and resources to help you get started. You can tailor your investments based on your knowledge and risk tolerance.

1. **Investing in Precious Metals (Gold, Silver):**

Precious metals like gold and silver have traditionally served as reliable investments. Their value tends to appreciate over time, and they also have utility in family events or special occasions. When buying gold, aim for pieces with more metal content and fewer artificial stones, as their value typically increases more over time.

1. **Investing in Businesses:**

If you have extra funds, consider investing in businesses—whether by starting your own or supporting a friend's venture. Many successful businesses have been built through capital borrowed from friends and family. You can formalize the agreement by defining ROI terms in a legal contract. This can be a highly rewarding, life-changing experience if done correctly. Stay informed about market trends, team capabilities, and other business factors before making an investment.

1. **Investing in Skills Upgradation:**

Lastly, one of the most valuable investments you can make is in your skills. Whether you're an employee or a business owner, upgrading your skills—or encouraging your employees to do so—ensures that you stay competitive in an ever-evolving marketplace. The time and money you invest in learning new skills will never be a loss; it will always provide returns in terms of career growth and opportunities.

By adopting any of these investment strategies, you're not only working towards financial freedom but also creating a secure, thriving future for yourself. Keep investing, learning, and adapting, and you will be well on your way to financial independence.

SECTION 2: INVESTING IN PAPER ASSETS

"Time well-spent results in more money to spend, more money to save, and more time to vacation."

-Zig Ziglar

6

Investing in Stocks/Shares

*"**N**ever rely on a single form of income. Consider making investments to create alternative income sources."*

-*Warren Buffett*

You've probably heard stories from friends or family about how they invested in a stock a few years ago and now it's worth five times more. It's easy to feel the impulse to jump in and try to reap similar benefits. However, many of us don't fully understand the basics of stock investing, and the fear of unexpected losses often holds us back.

I too had this urge some time ago. I decided to experiment with stock investments using money I could afford to lose, and I'm happy to report that those stocks have grown by 300% over time. Success! Now, I'm here to share this knowledge with you.

So, what exactly is a stock or share?

You may have heard about startups receiving investments from large Venture Capital (VC) firms to fuel their growth. But why do VCs invest in startups?

When startups are in their early stages, they have a lower market value. As the business grows and becomes more successful, its value increases. VCs invest at the early stages when the price is low, and later sell their shares when the market value rises (this is known as a "VC exit").

Similarly, when a company goes public through an Initial Public Offering (IPO), it releases shares to the public, offering anyone with an appetite for investing the chance to own a piece of the company. At the time of the IPO, the stock price may be low, allowing individuals from all walks of life to buy shares.

Stock investing works in much the same way. You invest in a company's stock and hold it for a while, eventually selling it for a profit. For the purpose of this discussion, we'll focus on long-term investing rather than short-term trading (such as intraday trading).

Stock Exchange: The Marketplace for Shares

All stocks are listed on a stock exchange, which serves as the marketplace where buyers and sellers transact. It's like a mall, but instead of shops selling clothes or electronics, the "stores" are different stocks.

To buy stocks, you'll need to open a trading account, either through your bank or platforms like Zerodha or Groww. (Note: Always ensure that these platforms are regulated by the government.)

Here's a simple flow of how stock purchasing works:

Seller → Demat Account → Stock Exchange → Buyer

A seller sells stocks via their demat account, and the buyer purchases them from the same stock exchange through their own demat account. The price of the stock is determined by supply and demand, and it remains fixed during the transaction — it's not negotiable.

When selecting stocks, there are various factors to consider: historical data, financial statements, price-to-earnings ratio (P/E ratio), and more. However, I'll share a personal tip that simplifies my approach:

Pro Tip: I buy stocks from companies I personally shop from. For example, I used to buy clothes from Tata-led brands, so I bought stocks in Tata clothing brands. During our house renovation, we used Asian Paints and Berger paints, so I invested in their stocks. Similarly, I ordered frequently from Zomato, so I bought shares of Zomato.

The idea is simple: If I'm already buying products from these companies because they offer good services, it may be worth owning a piece of them through stock investments. This way, you bypass endless analysis while investing in companies you believe in.

7

Investing in Mutual Funds

"There is a secret psychology of money. Most people don't know about it. That's why most people never become financially successful. A lack of money is not the problem; it is merely a symptom of what's going on inside of you."

-T. Harv Eker

You've likely seen the tagline "Mutual funds are subject to market risks." While this might make potential investors cautious, I believe it's important to understand the rules of the game, even if it involves risk. Let's break it down.

What is a mutual fund?

Investing in individual stocks can be risky. For example, a travel company's stock might plummet during a crisis like COVID-19. To mitigate this risk, you can diversify your investments by purchasing stocks across different industries or adding safer options like government bonds.

This is where mutual funds come in. They pool together investments in stocks, bonds, and other assets, spreading the risk across multiple sectors. When the value of these assets increases, so does the value of the mutual fund's units. The fund's price rises as it grows in value.

Mutual funds are categorized into three broad types based on the risk and return potential:

- **Equity Mutual Funds**
- **Debt Mutual Funds**
- **Hybrid Mutual Funds**

A new category, **Thematic Mutual Funds**, has also emerged, which we will discuss in more detail later.

Equity Mutual Funds

Equity mutual funds invest in stocks, which tend to have high risk and high returns. These funds are ideal for younger investors who can afford to ride out market volatility.

Typical returns range from 15-35% or more, but keep in mind that the market's ups and downs can significantly affect short-term performance.

Debt Mutual Funds

Debt funds invest in lower-risk assets like government bonds, which offer more stable returns. These funds are better suited for investors in older age groups who prefer security over high returns.

Expected returns generally fall in the range of 8-15%.

Hybrid Mutual Funds

Hybrid funds combine both equity and debt investments, offering a balanced approach. These funds typically appeal to individuals in their mid-life stages who are looking for moderate returns with moderate risk.

Returns typically range from 10-25%.

Systematic Investment Plan (SIP)

An SIP allows you to invest a fixed amount in mutual funds at regular intervals (such as monthly). This disciplined approach helps you build wealth over time.

Example: If you invest $10 monthly for a year, you would have $120 by the end of the year. With an average annual return of 8%, your investment could grow to around $125.60.

Systematic Withdrawal Plan (SWP)

An SWP is the opposite of SIP — you withdraw a fixed amount from your mutual fund investment regularly. It's a useful strategy for gradually using your savings without exhausting them too quickly.

Example: If you have $600 and choose to withdraw $50 monthly, you'll receive income for a year. Even if the investment grows at 6% annually, you'll still have some balance left after 12 months.

Equity-Linked Savings Scheme (ELSS)

An ELSS is a type of mutual fund that invests primarily in stocks. It offers the added benefit of tax savings but comes with the usual market risks. Additionally, it has a 3-year lock-in period.

Example: If you invest $100 in an ELSS with an expected return of 12%, your investment could grow to about $112 in one year. But remember, market fluctuations mean your returns can vary.

Fixed Deposit (FD)

An FD is a safer, low-risk option where you earn a fixed interest rate, whereas mutual funds can offer higher returns but with a higher level of risk.

FDs	
Safety	Guaranteed returns, very safe
Interest/Returns	Fixed interest rate
Tax Benefits	Interest is taxable based on your income tax slab
Flexibility	Fixed tenure, penalties for early withdrawal

Life Insurance

Insurance	
Purpose	Risk protection and coverage
Returns	Generally lower, guaranteed in some cases
Risk Level	Lower risk, guaranteed in some cases
Liquidity	Less liquid, long-term commitment

Term Insurance

	Term Insurance
Coverage	Pure life cover, no maturity benefits
Premium	Lower premiums
Duration	Fixed period
Benefits	Death benefit only

Each financial product serves different purposes:

- **Insurance products** focus on protection.
- **Mutual funds** are better for long-term wealth creation.
- **Fixed deposits** offer safety and guaranteed returns.
- **Term insurance** provides protection at lower costs.
- **Life insurance** combines protection with savings.

When choosing, align your decision with your:

- Financial goals
- Risk appetite
- Investment horizon
- Protection needs

Remember to review your portfolio regularly and adjust it based on your changing needs and market conditions.

The next chapters will delve into the technical aspects of investment and financial management, giving you an edge in making more informed decisions.

8

How to Perform Technical and Financial Analysis

"Money, like emotions, is something you must control to keep your life on the right track."

-Natasha Munson

Have you ever wondered how some investors seem to pick stocks with a magic touch? No, they don't have a crystal ball — they rely on technical and financial analysis. Let's explore how you can use these tools to become a savvy investor.

TECHNICAL ANALYSIS: READING THE MARKET'S MIND

Technical analysis is like being a detective, examining past market behavior to predict future trends. Here's how you can get started:

1. Chart Types: Visualizing Stock Movements

- **Line Charts**: Think of these as a "connect the dots" version of stock prices.
- **Bar Charts**: They show the price journey within a day, marking the open, high, low, and close.

- **Candlestick Charts**: These are like bar charts, but more colorful and easier to interpret.

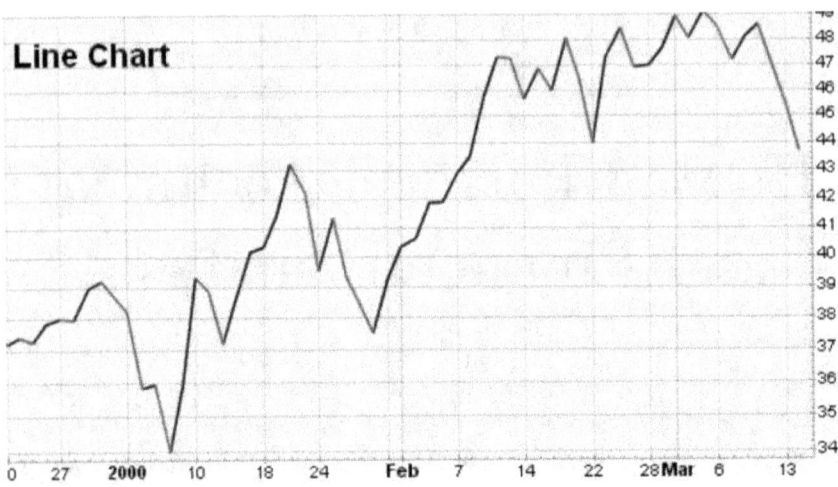

Figure 2: Line chart, Candlestick chart

Illustration: A dark candlestick indicates the stock closed higher than it opened, while a light one shows it closed lower.

2. Key Indicators: The Market's Mood Swings

- **Moving Averages (MA)**: Smooths out price movements over time, helping you spot trends.
- **Relative Strength Index (RSI)**: Think of it as a speedometer — above 70 means the stock may be overbought (slow down), and below 30 suggests it could be oversold (speed up).
- **MACD (Moving Average Convergence Divergence)**: Helps you spot buy or sell signals.
- **Bollinger Bands**: Like lanes on a highway, they show stock price volatility.

Illustration: If a stock price bounces off the upper Bollinger Band, it might be overbought — akin to a car hitting the lane markers.

3. Trends: Market Movements in Motion

- **Uptrend**: Think of a staircase, where each step is a higher high and higher low.
- **Downtrend**: Like a slide, with each step being a lower high and lower low.
- **Sideways Trend**: Like walking on a flat road, the price moves within a range.

4. Chart Patterns: The Market's Secret Messages

- **Head and Shoulders**: Indicates a trend reversal — like shrugging off a burden.
- **Double Top/Bottom**: Signals potential reversals — like hitting your head on the ceiling twice or bouncing on the floor.
- **Triangles**: Show continuation — like a flag waving in the wind.

5. Volume Analysis: The Market's Heartbeat

High volume on up days signals strength; on down days, it suggests weakness. Volume spikes often precede reversals, like a drumroll before a big event.

6. Support and Resistance: The Market's Boundaries

- **Support**: The floor where prices tend to bounce back up.
- **Resistance**: The ceiling where prices tend to hit a ceiling and fall back down.

Financial Analysis: Peering into the Company's Soul

Financial analysis helps you understand a company's health and true value. Here's how you can decode it:

1. Financial Statements: The Company's Report Card

- **Income Statement**: Reveals how much money the company made and spent — like a scorecard.
- **Balance Sheet**: A snapshot of what the company owns and owes.
- **Cash Flow Statement**: Tracks the flow of money in and out — like following a money trail.

Illustration: Think of the income statement as your monthly budget, the balance sheet as your wealth, and the cash flow statement as your cash on hand.

2. Financial Ratios: The Company's Vital Signs

- **Liquidity Ratios**: How easily the company can pay its bills.
    - *Current Ratio*: Current Assets / Current Liabilities

- *Quick Ratio*: (Current Assets - Inventory) / Current Liabilities
- **Profitability Ratios**: How well the company makes money.
  - *Gross Profit Margin*: (Revenue - COGS) / Revenue
  - *Net Profit Margin*: Net Income / Revenue
  - *ROA (Return on Assets)*: Net Income / Total Assets
  - *ROE (Return on Equity)*: Net Income / Shareholder's Equity
- **Leverage Ratios**: How much debt the company uses.
  - *Debt-to-Equity Ratio*: Total Debt / Shareholder's Equity
  - *Interest Coverage Ratio*: EBIT / Interest Expenses
- **Efficiency Ratios**: How effectively the company uses its resources.
  - *Inventory Turnover*: COGS / Average Inventory
  - *Asset Turnover*: Revenue / Total Assets

Illustration: Liquidity ratios are like your ability to pay off a surprise bill, profitability ratios are how well you turn a lemonade stand into profit, and leverage ratios show how much you owe vs. what you own.

3. Growth Metrics: The Company's Growth Spurt

- **Revenue Growth**: Like tracking your allowance increases over the years.
- **Earnings Growth**: Watching your piggy bank grow as you save more each month.

4. Valuation Ratios: The Company's Price Tag

- **P/E Ratio (Price-to-Earnings)**: Current stock price / EPS
- **P/B Ratio (Price-to-Book)**: Current stock price / Book value per share

- **P/S Ratio (Price-to-Sales)**: Current stock price / Revenue per share

Illustration: Think of the P/E ratio as comparing the price of a candy bar to its taste rating — is it worth the price?

5. Cash Flow: The Company's Lifeblood

Positive cash flow from operations means the company can sustain its business. *Free Cash Flow*: Operating Cash Flow - Capital Expenditures.

Illustration: Cash flow is like the money you have left after paying all your expenses — what can you do with it?

6. Qualitative Factors: The Company's Character

- **Management Quality**: Strong leaders make a big difference.
- **Industry Position**: Is the company a leader or a follower?
- **Economic Moat**: Does it have a unique advantage over competitors?

Combining Technical and Financial Analysis: The Dynamic Duo

1. Confirm Signals:

Use technical analysis to find entry and exit points, and validate with financial analysis to ensure the company is fundamentally strong.

2. Risk Management:

Set stop-loss and take-profit levels with technical analysis. Financial analysis helps you understand the company's risk factors.

3. Continuous Monitoring:

Regularly update both analyses to stay informed about changes.

Illustration: Think of technical analysis as the weather forecast and financial analysis as building a strong house. Together, they help you navigate the stock market storm!

9

How to Manage Your Personal Finances

"Money moves from those who do not manage it to those who do."

-Dave Ramsey

Managing personal finances doesn't have to be complicated. Think of it as a game where your goal is to make money work for you. Here's how to become a financial wizard in simple steps!

1. Set Clear Financial Goals
Before managing your money, you need clear goals. These can be short-term, medium-term, or long-term.
Examples:

- **Short-term**: Save $100 a month for a new gadget.
- **Medium-term**: Save $1,000 for a vacation next year.
- **Long-term**: Save for college or a car down payment.

Tip: Write down your goals and keep them visible daily.

2. Create a Budget

A budget is like a map for your money. It shows where your money is going and helps you make adjustments.

Steps:

- **List Income**: Include all sources of money.
- **Track Expenses**: Write down everything you spend money on.
- **Categorize Expenses**: Divide into needs (food, transportation) and wants (entertainment, dining out).
- **Set Limits**: Allocate amounts for each category.

Example:

- **Income**: $200/month
- **Needs**: $100
- **Wants**: $50
- **Savings**: $50

Tip: Use budgeting apps or spreadsheets to track.

3. Save Regularly

Saving is like planting a tree — it grows over time. Set aside a portion of your income regularly.

Types of savings:

- **Emergency Fund**: 3-6 months of living expenses.
- **Short-term Savings**: For upcoming expenses.
- **Long-term Savings**: For big future goals.

Tip: Start small if needed. Even $10/month adds up.

4. Reduce and Manage Debt

Debt isn't bad, but too much can be overwhelming. Here's how to manage it:

- **Know What You Owe**: List all debts.
- **Prioritize Payments**: Pay high-interest debts first.
- **Create a Plan**: Fit payments into your budget.

Example: If your credit card debt has 18% interest, pay it off first before tackling a student loan with 5% interest.

Tip: Avoid new debt unless necessary.

5. Invest Wisely

Investing is like making your money work for you. Start early to see the benefits.

Types of Investments:

- **Stocks**: High potential returns, higher risk.
- **Bonds**: Lower risk, lower returns.
- **Mutual Funds**: Diversified portfolio of stocks and bonds.

Tip: Start with low-cost options like index funds.

6. Protect Your Finances

Insurance and emergency planning protect your financial health.

Types of Insurance:

- **Health Insurance**: Covers medical expenses.
- **Auto Insurance**: Covers car accidents.
- **Home Insurance**: Protects your home.

Emergency Planning:

- **Emergency Fund**: For unexpected expenses.
- **Will**: To ensure assets are distributed as per your wishes.

Tip: Review insurance policies annually.

7. Keep Learning

Financial management is a lifelong journey. Stay informed and adjust as life changes.

Resources:

- **Books**: "Rich Dad Poor Dad" by Robert Kiyosaki, "The Total Money Makeover" by Dave Ramsey.
- **Online Courses**: Websites like Coursera and Khan Academy offer free finance courses.
- **Podcasts and Blogs**: Follow experts who share insights.

Tip: Review your finances monthly and keep learning.

Conclusion

This book is a guide to mastering both your personal finances and investing in paper assets. From setting goals and budgeting to mastering stock analysis, each chapter provides tools that have transformed my own financial journey. With dedication, these tools can make a profound impact on your financial life as well. Happy managing!

www.ingramcontent.com/pod-product-compliance
Lightning Source LLC
LaVergne TN
LVHW010615070526
838199LV00063BA/5158